Bub Can Sing

By Sally Cowan

Sim hung on a branch.

He had a peck
at some buds.

Then, Sim sang a song.

"What is that song?"
said Bub.

"Sim wants me to sip
with him," said Pim.

"Can I sip, too?" said Bub.

"Not yet, Bub!" said Pim.
"Chicks can not go off
to sip."

Bub put up his wings.

I am not such a little chick.
Look at my long wings!

Pim checked Bub's wings.

Can you flap them?

Bub did a little flap.

Then, he did a big, big flap!

Bub went up, up, up
to the top branch.

"Let's go, Bub!" said Pim.

When Pim and Bub
got to Sim,
Sim looked at Bub's wings.

What long wings Bub has!

Then, Bub had a big sip.

"Sip, sip!" sang Bub.
"Sip, sip!"

Bub can sing so well!

CHECKING FOR MEANING

1. Why did Sim sing a song? *(Literal)*

2. How did Bub get up to the top branch? *(Literal)*

3. Why is Bub able to fly now? *(Inferential)*

EXTENDING VOCABULARY

hung	What does *hung* mean in this story? Can you find other *–ng* words in the story? What other *–ng* words can you make? Which sounds go before *–ng* in these words?
such	What sound do the letters *–ch* make in this word? Share a sentence with a partner that contains a word ending in *–ch.* Ask your partner to identify the word, and then change roles.
checked	How many sounds are in this word? What are they? How does adding *–ed* to the end of the word *check* change its meaning? What other words do you know that have *–ed* at the end?

MOVING BEYOND THE TEXT

1. Where do baby birds live when they are very young?

2. What do baby birds eat? How do they get food?

3. How do baby birds learn to fly?

4. When do baby birds leave their mother's nest?

SPEED SOUNDS

| sh | ch | th | th | ck | ng |

voiced   unvoiced

branch

hung

peck

song

sang

with

chick

Chicks

checked

such

wings

long